American Moments

ABDO & Daughters

THE BOMBING OF PEARL HARBOR

By Alan Pierce

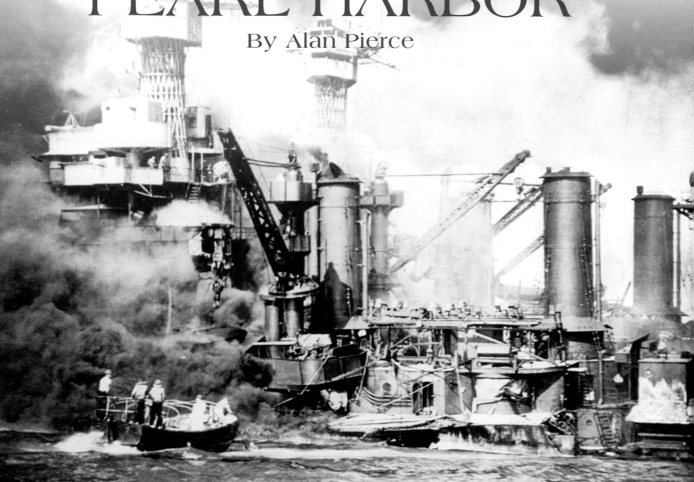

VISIT US AT
WWW.ABDOPUB.COM

Published by ABDO Publishing Company, 4940 Viking Drive, Suite 622, Edina, Minnesota 55435. Copyright © 2005 by Abdo Consulting Group, Inc. International copyrights reserved in all countries. No part of this book may be reproduced in any form without written permission from the publisher. ABDO & Daughters™ is a trademark and logo of ABDO Publishing Company.

Printed in the United States.

Edited by: Melanie A. Howard
Interior Production and Design: Terry Dunham Incorporated
Cover Design: Mighty Media
Photos: Corbis, Library of Congress, U.S. Navy

Library of Congress Cataloging-in-Publication Data

Pierce, Alan, 1966-
    The bombing of Pearl Harbor / Alan Pierce.
        p. cm. -- (American moments)
    Includes index.
    ISBN 1-59197-729-0
    1. Pearl Harbor (Hawaii), Attack on, 1941--Juvenile literature. 2. World War, 1939-1945--Causes--Juvenile literature. I. Title. II. Series.

D767.92.P54 2004
940.54'26693--dc22
                                                                            2004054337

CONTENTS

AIR RAID ON PEARL HARBOR

On December 7, 1941, the weather was beautiful at Pearl Harbor, Hawaii. High clouds shared the sky with the sun. Thousands of U.S. sailors and troops were stationed at Pearl Harbor because it was the home of the U.S. Pacific Fleet. On that Sunday morning, they started their different activities. Some ate breakfast on navy ships or at bases around the harbor. Others headed to church services.

Many sailors were also in the harbor. They participated in ceremonies to raise the American flags aboard the ships. Some men saw airplanes approaching. The bombers were flying so low that the Americans saw a pilot wave. Someone on a battleship shouted that the planes must be Soviet because of the red ball design on the aircraft. At this time, the United States was aiding the Soviet Union in a war against Germany.

The red ball design, however, did not indicate Soviet airplanes. Instead, the ball represented the sun found on the Japanese flag. At 7:55 AM, Japanese planes unleashed their bombs and torpedoes on U.S. ships in Pearl Harbor. Within minutes, radio operators relayed the message, "Air raid on Pearl Harbor. This is no drill."

This message alerted other U.S. forces and leaders in Washington DC about the attack. But the message also announced that the United States had entered the combat of World War II. For years,

During the attack on Pearl Harbor, the USS California
is hit while the USS Oklahoma *capsizes.*

the United States had tried to avoid war with Japan. But the swarms
of Japanese planes and the destruction of the ships in Pearl Harbor
showed that war was now a reality for the United States.

PROGRESS IN JAPAN

Japan had not always been a threat to other countries. At one time, Japan had mostly closed itself off from the rest of the world. In the 1630s, Japanese military leaders called shoguns barred almost all foreigners from entering the country. The shoguns were wary of Christian missionaries from Europe. People in Japan mainly practiced the Buddhist and Shinto religions. The Christian missionaries wanted to convert the Japanese to Christianity. The shoguns feared the missionaries might clear the way for a European conquest of Japan.

Despite Japan's policy, European and U.S. warships went to Japan in the 1840s. The Europeans and Americans wanted to open up Japan for trade. In July 1853, U.S. commodore Matthew C. Perry led a fleet of warships into a Japanese port called Uraga. Perry demanded trade and the use of Japanese

Commodore Matthew C. Perry visits Japanese officials while negotiating a trade agreement.

Japan in the nineteenth century.

ports, or the United States would go to war with Japan. Within a year, Japan agreed to U.S. terms in the Treaty of Kanagawa.

Soon, other nations began making treaties with Japan. The sudden presence of these foreigners weakened the power of the shoguns. One of the shoguns' reasons for holding power was that they kept foreigners out of Japan. They could no longer make this claim.

Eventually, armies opposed to the shoguns occupied the imperial palace in the city of Kyōto. On January 3, 1868, these forces announced that the emperor now led the government. At this time, the emperor was a 15-year-old boy named Mutsuhito. With the collapse of the shoguns, the emperor and his supporters now governed Japan.

The new government was committed to changing Japan into a modern nation. In this way, Japanese leaders hoped to compete with the United States and European countries. The nation began building telegraph lines and railroads. By 1872, Japan's first railroad line connected the cities of Yokohama and Tokyo. During the next few years, thousands of miles of railroad tracks were built in Japan.

Politics, as well as technology, was undergoing rapid change in Japan. Many people began to demand a constitution. Those who supported a constitution were influenced by ideas from western Europe and the United States. It seemed to some Japanese that constitutions made these nations stronger. Moreover, many people also wanted an elected assembly in Japan.

On February 11, 1889, the government announced that it was giving a constitution to the Japanese people. The constitution created an assembly called the Diet to pass laws. The Diet was made up of two chambers called the House of Representatives and the House of Peers. But the constitution provided for little supervision over the military. Only the emperor had authority over Japan's armed forces.

Opposite page: Emperor Mutsuhito's rule became known as the Meiji period. It was characterized by political, social, and technological change in Japan.

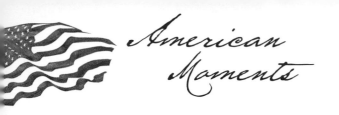
NEW POWERS IN THE PACIFIC

Japan had undergone great change in the nineteenth century. The nation was no longer shut off from the rest of the world. It was also in a stronger position to stand up to other countries. In the 1880s and 1890s, Japan began to spend more money to strengthen its navy and army. Furthermore, Japan began to compete with other powers in the region for influence in eastern Asia.

The nation of Korea was of special interest to Japan. Some leaders believed that control of this nearby country was important for Japan's security. Japan competed with China for influence in Korea. This rivalry led to the Sino-Japanese War in 1894. A rebellion in Korea gave Japan an excuse to send thousands of troops to the country. The Japanese government said it wanted to protect Japanese citizens living in Korea. Fighting, however, soon broke out between Japanese and Chinese forces.

Japan inflicted heavy losses on Chinese forces. The Treaty of Shimonoseki ended the war in April 1895. Under the treaty, Japan gained many concessions from China. Japan received Taiwan and the Liaodong Peninsula in Manchuria. In addition, Japan acquired the right to build railroads in southern Manchuria.

Meanwhile, the United States emerged as an important power in the Pacific Ocean. The event that transformed the United States was the

The explosion of the USS Maine *killed 260 sailors.*

Spanish-American War in 1898. The Spanish colony of Cuba revolted against Spain. Cuba's fight for independence received the support of the United States. On February 15, 1898, an explosion sank the USS *Maine* in Cuba's Havana harbor. The cause of the explosion was never determined, but U.S. newspapers blamed Spain.

In April, the two countries went to war. On May 1, the United States attacked the Philippines, which was a Spanish colony. After destroying the Spanish fleet in Manila Bay, the United States defeated Spanish warships in the Caribbean Sea. By July, the war was over. In the Treaty of Paris, the United States acquired the Philippines and Guam in the Pacific Ocean, and Puerto Rico in the Caribbean Sea. A U.S. military government ruled Cuba.

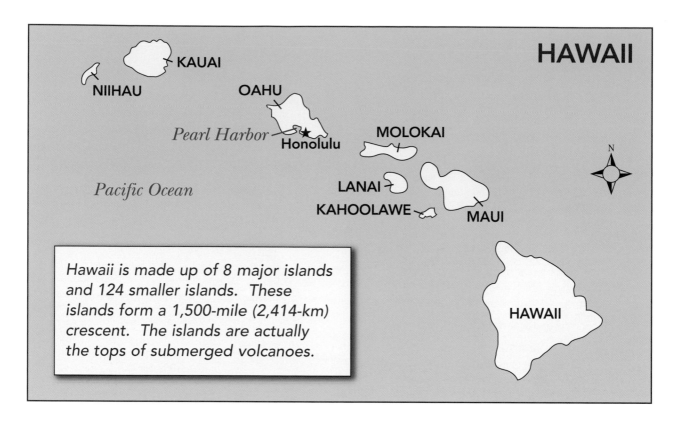

At this time, the United States also gained control of Hawaii. For many decades, the United States had maintained contact with the people in Hawaii. Christian missionaries and whaling ships had long visited the island. In 1893, an American named Sanford Dole led a group that overthrew Hawaii's Queen Liliuokalani. The new government wanted the United States to take over the island. On July 7, 1898, the United States annexed Hawaii.

After the United States gained territories in the Pacific Ocean, Japan secured its position in Asia. The main threat to Japanese interests in Korea and Manchuria was Russia. A treaty made in 1902 obligated Russia to remove its troops from Manchuria. Japan asked Russia to abide by this agreement, but Russia refused. On February 8, 1904, Japan carried out a surprise attack against Russian ships at

Port Arthur on the Manchurian coast. This attack began the Russo-Japanese War.

Japan won several victories against Russia. One important victory occurred in the Battle of Tsushima. On May 27, 1905, the Japanese navy attacked a Russian fleet in the Tsushima Strait between the islands of Kyūshū and Tsushima. In the two-day battle, the Japanese sank and captured several Russian ships while suffering few losses.

Japan's victories, however, were draining the country. The war was expensive, and Japan had suffered many casualties. Japanese leaders asked U.S. president Theodore Roosevelt to hold peace talks between Russia and Japan. Roosevelt agreed, which led to the Treaty of Portsmouth in 1905. The treaty awarded the Liaodong Peninsula and South Manchurian Railway to Japan. Japan also received recognition for its domination of Korea and acquired half of Sakhalin Island.

The Russo-Japanese War was also important for reasons other than Japan's territorial acquisitions. For the first time in modern history, an Asian nation had defeated a European power. Japan received the respect of European countries.

Theodore Roosevelt

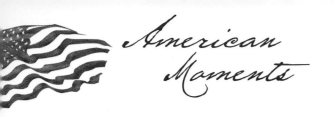

JAPAN'S GROWING MIGHT

The United States and Japan were not the only colonial powers in eastern Asia. By the early twentieth century, some European countries had colonized large areas of the continent. Britain controlled Burma, which is now called Myanmar, and India. The British also governed the area that is now the nation of Malaysia. France ruled a region in Southeast Asia called French Indochina. This area now makes up the countries of Cambodia, Laos, and Vietnam. The Netherlands controlled modern-day Indonesia. This colony was known as the Dutch East Indies.

Many of these colonies were rich in resources. Indochina produced rice, coal, and rubber. India possessed productive coalfields. This coal supply helped form a steel industry in India. The East Indies became an important supplier of rubber and oil.

After Japan's victory in the Russo-Japanese War, many Asians saw Japan as a nation opposed to colonialism. Japan, however, made alliances with European colonial powers such as Britain and France. In 1914, when World War I broke out, Japan was allied with Britain. Germany was Britain's enemy in the war. As Britain's ally, Japan captured German possessions in China's Shandong Peninsula.

China requested the return of this land. Japan refused. In 1915, Japan issued the Twenty-one Demands. These demands called for

ASIAN COLONIES IN 1914

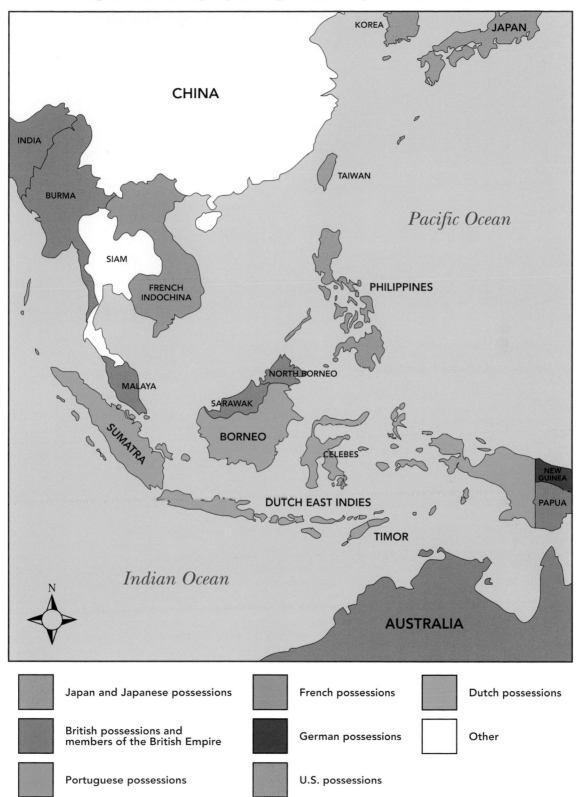

KOREA

JAPAN

CHINA

INDIA

TAIWAN

BURMA

Pacific Ocean

SIAM

FRENCH
INDOCHINA

PHILIPPINES

MALAYA

NORTH BORNEO

SARAWAK

SUMATRA

BORNEO

CELEBES

NEW
GUINEA

DUTCH EAST INDIES

PAPUA

TIMOR

Indian Ocean

N

AUSTRALIA

Japan and Japanese possessions	French possessions	Dutch possessions	
British possessions and members of the British Empire	German possessions	Other	
Portuguese possessions	U.S. possessions		

China to agree to Japan's control of the land in the Shandong Peninsula. In addition, the Twenty-one Demands asked China to include Japanese advisors in the Chinese government.

The Chinese people were furious about the Twenty-one Demands. China asked European nations for help, but Europe was engaged in war and was in no position to become seriously involved. Eventually, the Chinese government agreed to some of Japan's demands. China accepted Japan's control of the Shandong Peninsula and southern Manchuria.

World War I contributed to another conflict that affected Japan and other countries. Russia was at war with Germany, as well. But Russia's army performed poorly against German forces. These failures caused many Russians to resent their leader, Czar Nicholas II. Eventually, groups hostile to the czar overthrew his government in the Russian Revolution.

A revolutionary leader named Vladimir Lenin came to power in Russia in 1917. Lenin had been influenced by Karl Marx's theories. Marx was a German thinker who wrote about conflict between workers and those who were more powerful than the workers. His theories predicted a revolution in which the workers would overthrow the people in power. This revolution would eliminate rich and poor classes of people. Marx's ideas gave rise to communism.

Lenin angered Britain, France, and the United States by agreeing to a peace treaty with Germany in March 1918. This treaty affected the United States because America had entered the war against Germany one year earlier. After Russia made peace, Germany could focus its army on the United States, Britain, and France.

In early 1918, Britain, France, the United States, and Japan sent troops to Siberia. These troops arrived to help forces that were still

Vladimir Lenin

Karl Marx

loyal to the czar. By the time the war ended in 1918, these forces were still unsuccessful. Most countries withdrew their troops from Siberia. Japan, however, kept its forces there until 1922. The continuation of Japanese troops in Siberia created worries about Japan's ambitions.

In 1921 and 1922, the victorious powers from the war held meetings to create more stability in East Asia. These meetings in Washington DC produced the Five-Power Naval Limitation Treaty in February 1922. The treaty allowed the United States and Britain to have a larger naval force than Japan. However, Japan was permitted a larger fleet than Italy or France. The Japanese people scorned the restrictions placed on their country. Nevertheless, Japan accepted the treaty because the United States and Britain agreed not to increase their naval fortifications in the western Pacific.

FASCISM

The Five-Power Naval Limitation Treaty indicated a willingness to settle disagreements peacefully after World War I. But one political movement led some countries toward violence. This movement was called fascism. It began in Italy under the leadership of Benito Mussolini. Fascism promoted strong beliefs in nationalism. In Italy, Mussolini worked to identify Italy with the glory of the Roman Empire.

Many Italians were bitter about World War I. The country had been victorious, but 600,000 Italians had died in the war. Also, many people saw their government as weak. This feeling of resentment allowed Mussolini to come to power in 1922. Once Mussolini became the leader of Italy, he worked toward becoming a dictator.

A propaganda poster of Benito Mussolini

In the 1920s, Japan followed a different path than Italy. Japan became more democratic. The country allowed all males older than 25 to vote. In foreign relations, Japan stressed greater cooperation with other nations. For example, it encouraged more trade with the United States, Europe, and the rest of Asia.

On the other hand, Japanese society had ideas that were opposed to democracy and peace. Since the late nineteenth century, many Japanese schoolchildren had been taught that the emperor was divine. Consequently, Japanese students learned that obeying the emperor was a person's most important duty. Another important belief was that Japan was superior to other nations. As a great nation, it was Japan's responsibility to liberate Asia from European and U.S. control.

Japan also had another reason for expanding its territory. The country's population was increasing, especially in the cities. A growing population created more demand for resources, which Japan lacked. Territorial expansion was seen as one solution to Japan's population growth. More territory could provide Japan's people with more resources.

In 1929, a depression crippled economies throughout the world. This economic calamity was called the Great Depression in the United

Pea pickers face hardship in Nipomo, California, during the Great Depression.

States. The economic collapse put millions of Americans out of work and caused thousands of banks to fail.

The global depression also had major consequences for Japan. Factories closed and unemployment soared in the cities. Many Japanese began to lose their confidence in democracy, which had not

Tsuyoshi Inukai (right) *succeeded Wakatsuki Reijiro as prime minister of Japan.*

prevented the depression. Fascism began to seem more appealing to the Japanese. In addition, some believed the Depression required a military solution.

In the early 1930s, Japan's military began to control the country's foreign policy. In September 1931, the Japanese military took control of Manchuria and set up a government under Japanese rule. Eventually, Japan sent 500,000 colonists to settle in Manchuria. Japanese prime minister Tsuyoshi Inukai attempted to restrain the military. However, a group of naval officers assassinated the prime minister in 1932.

Soon, Germany emerged as another fascist country. Many Germans were bitter about their defeat in World War I. After the war, Germans experienced severe economic hardship when their money became worthless. The country's economy eventually recovered, but the depression that devastated much of the world also hurt Germany. Millions of Germans were out of work. Under these conditions, the fascist Nazi Party was able to rise to power. The party's leader was Adolf Hitler.

German and Italian fascism had much in common. Like Mussolini in Italy, Hitler eventually became a dictator. Both German Nazism and Italian fascism were extremely nationalistic. Fascists in both countries hated the Marxist beliefs that had taken hold in the Soviet Union.

Hatred of communism was one point that drew Germany and Japan together. On November 25, 1936, both countries signed the Anti-Comintern Pact. This treaty committed Germany and Japan to oppose the Soviet Union by sharing information. Japan was angry with the Soviet Union, which was selling weapons to China.

Benito Mussolini (left) and Adolf Hitler in Munich, Germany.

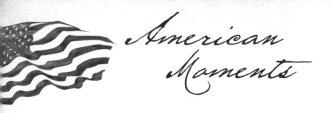

American Moments

THE LOOMING CRISIS

Serious fighting broke out between Japan and China in July 1937. Japanese troops near the Marco Polo Bridge near Beijing reported being fired upon by Chinese forces. A wider war soon broke out as Japan sent more troops into China. Japan attacked major Chinese cities, such as Shanghai and Nanking. In Nanking, Japanese forces massacred thousands of Chinese people and plundered the city. No one is sure how many were killed, although Chinese sources place the number at more than 300,000 people.

The United States condemned Japan's war with China. But there was not much the United States was willing to do to oppose Japan. In the 1930s, many Americans believed in isolationism. This called for the United States to stay out of international disputes, especially in Europe. The experience of World War I led some Americans to adopt this policy. The isolationists concluded that U.S. involvement in that war had been a mistake. They did not want to repeat the error by getting involved in another war.

Many members of the U.S. Congress shared this view. Under the influence of isolationism, Congress passed laws intended to keep the United States out of wars. For example, Congress outlawed the sale of weapons to nations at war.

Famous aviator Charles Lindbergh was a prominent isolationist. Here he is speaking at an America First rally. America First was a powerful isolationist group before World War II.

While many Americans were isolationists, their president was not. President Franklin D. Roosevelt believed the United States should become involved in international problems. Roosevelt was concerned about the ambitions of Japan and Nazi Germany. On September 1, 1939, Germany invaded Poland, triggering World War II in Europe. Britain and France were committed to defending Poland, but the United States stayed out of the war.

Meanwhile, Japan's war against China continued. The United States wanted Japan to withdraw its forces from China. In order to compel Japan to do so, the United States stopped selling scrap iron, premium steel, and aviation gasoline to Japan.

At this time, Japan relied on the United States for many resources. For example, the United States supplied 80 percent of Japan's oil. U.S. leaders believed the decision to halt oil sales to Japan would lead to war between the two countries.

In 1940, German armies conquered France and the Netherlands. Japan began to covet the Asian colonies of these defeated nations. The resources in these colonies, such as rubber and petroleum, would aid Japan's military. In September 1940, Japan, Germany, and Italy signed the Tripartite Pact. This treaty obligated the three countries to defend each other if they were attacked. Moreover, the treaty suggested that the United States was their mutual enemy.

In July 1941, President Roosevelt announced that the United States was freezing Japanese assets in the United States. Japan could still trade with the United States, but any trade would have to be approved by the U.S. government. However, Roosevelt's order was misunderstood by government officials. They treated the president's decision as a total cutoff of trade between the United

States and Japan. Roosevelt did not try to fix the mistake for fear of looking weak.

The United States had cut off Japan's main source of oil. So, Japanese leaders began to prepare for war. At this time, Japan's government had undergone an important change. Tōjō Hideki had become prime minister. Tōjō had been an army general, and he had served as the minister of war. He believed Japan must go to war to maintain its empire.

Japanese leaders called for capturing the oilfields in the Dutch East Indies. To be successful, the Japanese military knew it must also attack U.S. forces in the Philippines and British forces in Singapore. They would also need to destroy the U.S. Pacific Fleet at Pearl Harbor.

Romanian prime minister Ion Antonescu meets with
Adolf Hitler to sign the Tripartite Pact in November 1940

PREPARING FOR THE ATTACK

Japan's leaders believed they had little time to spare. The country's navy estimated that Japan's oil reserves would last only 18 months. Japan hoped that a sudden, devastating strike on Pearl Harbor would stun the United States. America would then give Japan the freedom to carry out its war in Asia. Few Japanese leaders believed their country could win a long war against the United States.

The man who planned the attack on Pearl Harbor was Admiral Yamamoto Isoroku, a veteran of the battle of Tsushima. Yamamoto did not want to fight the United States. He had studied and worked in the United States, and he knew about the country's potential strength.

Despite his concerns, Yamamoto dedicated himself to planning the attack. The attack presented the Japanese with many challenges. More than 3,500 miles (5,633 km) of ocean separated Japan from Pearl Harbor. This vast distance would make it difficult for the Japanese force to refuel. Also, there was a chance that such a large force might be discovered. Japanese military planners set up a model of Pearl Harbor in Saeki Bay. They practiced the attack on a game board at Japan's Naval War College.

By late November, Japan had assembled its naval and air forces for the attack. Admiral Nagumo Chuichi led the fleet. The force included

Admiral Yamamoto Isoroku

Admiral Nagumo Chuichi

JAPAN'S FLEET

The six aircraft carriers that Japan sent to attack Pearl Harbor were the Akagi, Hiryu, Kaga, Soryu, Shokaku, and Zuikaku. The Akagi (top right) was one of Japan's first two aircraft carriers. It was built in Kure, Japan. The ship was later bombed by U.S. forces at the Battle of Midway in June 1942, along with the Hiryu, Soryu, and Kaga. U.S. forces bombed the Zuikaku (bottom right) and Shokaku a month earlier in the Battle of the Coral Sea.

more than 30 ships. Six aircraft carriers, two battleships, several cruisers and destroyers, and eight oil tankers made up the fleet. In addition, the force included more than 400 airplanes and more than 20 submarines.

On November 26, 1941, the Japanese force set out from Japan. The fleet traveled in complete radio silence to avoid detection. Japanese sailors used flags and lamps to communicate among the ships. By December 6, Nagumo's fleet was located more than 230 miles (370 km) north of Oahu. Commander Fuchida Mitsuo was assigned to lead the first group of warplanes over Pearl Harbor.

Japanese planes prepare for the attack on Pearl Harbor.

Pearl Harbor is located on the island of Oahu in the Hawaiian Islands. The harbor is commonly described as clover shaped. The stem forms the entrance from the Pacific Ocean into the harbor. Lochs branch off from the entrance to form the "leaves" of the clover. Ford Island is situated among these lochs. The harbor provides about 10 square miles (26 sq km) of navigable water.

Other military bases were located on Oahu as well. Hickam Field was east of Pearl Harbor. This base served as the U.S. military's chief airfield in Hawaii. West of Pearl Harbor lay Ewa Marine Corps Air Station. Another base, Wheeler Field, occupied the center of the island. On the eastern side of Oahu were the Kaneohe Naval Air Station and Bellows Field. All of these bases offered the Japanese many targets.

PEARL HARBOR, HAWAII
DECEMBER 7, 1941

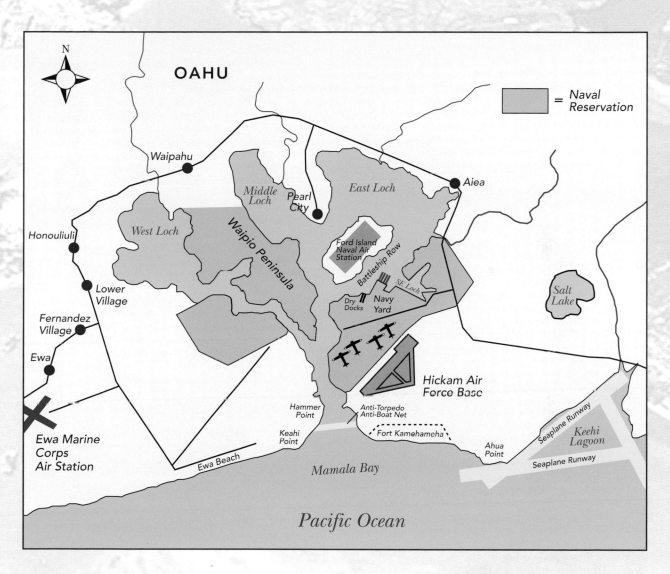

DECEMBER 7, 1941

On December 7, 1941, more than 90 warships in the U.S. Pacific Fleet were in Pearl Harbor. The fleet included the battleships *Arizona*, *California*, *Maryland*, *Nevada*, *Oklahoma*, *Pennsylvania*, *Tennessee*, and *West Virginia*. All the battleships but the *Pennsylvania* were arranged along the east side of Ford Island. This area near Ford Island was known as Battleship Row. The *Pennsylvania* was south of Battleship Row in dry dock.

But some important ships were not at Pearl Harbor that day. The aircraft carriers of the U.S. Pacific Fleet had sailed from the harbor. The USS *Enterprise* and USS *Lexington* had recently left to take airplanes to Wake and Midway islands. They were both more than 200 miles (322 km) away. The USS *Saratoga* had gone to the U.S. mainland for repairs and to transport airplanes back to Pearl Harbor.

The Japanese had taken great care to conceal their attack. However, there were warnings that an attack was imminent. At 3:57 AM, an officer aboard the minesweeper *Condor* reported a suspicious sight near the harbor's entrance. He spotted the periscope of a submarine. The destroyer *Ward* used sonar to search for a submarine, but found nothing.

Less than three hours later, men aboard the *Ward* and the supply ship *Antares* saw a curious sight outside the harbor's entrance. They spotted an object that looked like a submarine. No submarines were allowed in this area without permission. The *Ward* fired at the

These Japanese bombers are the same type of planes that attacked Pearl Harbor.

submarine and dropped bombs called depth charges. Before 7:00 AM, the *Ward*'s commanding officer, Lieutenant William W. Outerbridge, reported the incident. The navy, however, did not inform the army.

At 7:00 AM, army radar operators on Oahu noticed a strange reading. The radar indicated that many aircraft from the north were heading toward the island. This pack of aircraft was Fuchida's warplanes. However, an officer named Kermit Tyler didn't think the reading was unusual. He believed the radar had picked up the arrival of U.S. B-17 Flying Fortress bombers. Tyler told the operators to ignore the reading.

At 7:40 AM, Fuchida fired a flare from his cockpit as a signal for the pilots to fall into attack formation. Some pilots failed to respond, so Fuchida fired a second flare. This caused some confusion because two flares meant that surprise had not been achieved. Nevertheless, the attack proceeded.

Despite the confusion of the other pilots, Fuchida believed the Americans were unaware of the impending attack. At 7:53 AM, he yelled the Japanese word for tiger into his radio, *"Tora! Tora! Tora!"* This message alerted the Japanese carrier force that Fuchida's planes had achieved total surprise. With surprise achieved at Pearl Harbor, Japan could now launch attacks against the Philippines and throughout Southeast Asia.

At 7:55 AM, the Japanese bombers struck the U.S. Pacific Fleet. Torpedoes hit the *West Virginia* and *Oklahoma*. Bombers also attacked the old battleship *Utah*, which was used for training.

Bombers armed with shells designed to blast through decks swooped toward the *Arizona*. One bomb detonated in the area where the battleship stored its ammunition. The explosion destroyed the *Arizona* and hurled fire and smoke 500 feet (152 m) into the air. More than 1,100 men died in the attack. About 300 survivors managed to swim away or board rescue ships.

Japanese bombers and fighters struck against other bases. They attacked Hickam Field for only ten minutes, but they caused tremendous damage. Many of the planes lined up on the ground were destroyed. Afterward, 182 men were dead or missing. Wheeler Field, Ewa Marine Corps Air Station, and Kaneohe Naval Air Station also suffered attacks.

The first wave of attacks ended at about 8:30 AM. Japanese forces had killed thousands of U.S. military personnel and destroyed or

PEARL HARBOR CONTROVERSY

Franklin D. Roosevelt

Some historians believe that President Franklin D. Roosevelt deliberately provoked the attack on Pearl Harbor. These historians argue that Roosevelt wanted the United States to enter World War II to help Britain against Germany. However, Roosevelt knew the American people were unlikely to support this effort. Only an attack on the United States would arouse public support for a war.

Supporters of this theory argue that Roosevelt was preparing to go to war. For example, the president called for a plan to draft men into the military during peacetime. Also, he asked Congress to allow the United States to sell weapons to Britain and France.

Those who support this theory also point to Roosevelt's policy toward Japan. They claim the U.S. embargo against Japan was an attempt to involve the United States in a war. These historians say that Roosevelt and several American policy makers knew this action would provoke a Japanese attack.

The experts' strongest argument, however, is U.S. knowledge about Japan's intentions. By December 7, Japanese messages indicating an attack had been decoded. These decoded messages were not shared with the military. Despite these accusations, however, most historians believe that Roosevelt was just as surprised as the rest of the nation when Pearl Harbor was attacked.

damaged several ships and airplanes. In contrast, Japan had lost only nine planes.

The second wave of Japanese airplanes arrived at 8:55 AM. Lieutenant Commander Shimazaki Shigekazu led this group of bombers and fighters. The planes swept in from the northeast to hit the airfields and Pearl Harbor again.

By this time, U.S. military personnel were able to put up a better defense. Pilots were able to get a few P-40 and P-36 airplanes into the air. U.S. pilots managed to shoot down 13 Japanese aircraft. Also, U.S. soldiers and navy personnel began returning fire with anti-aircraft guns.

Despite these efforts, the Japanese still inflicted damage. At Pearl Harbor, bombers set upon the *Nevada* as the battleship attempted to reach the ocean. The ship's captain decided to run the *Nevada* ashore rather than risk blocking the harbor's entrance with a damaged ship. Planes also hit the *Pennsylvania*, killing several men and wounding 38 others.

By 9:45 AM, the second wave had finished its attack. The Japanese bombers left behind a terrible scene of destruction. Smoke poured from burning ships in Pearl Harbor. The wounded filled the hospital on Ford Island. In fact, the number of wounded was so large that injured people were treated at barracks and mess halls, as well. More than 2,300 Americans were killed in the attack, or died later from their wounds. Another 1,178 were injured. At least 49 civilians were killed in the attack.

The United States also suffered staggering losses to its ships and planes. Japanese bombers sank or damaged the eight battleships. Other destroyers and cruisers were also sunk or damaged. In addition,

The USS Arizona Memorial was built over the sunken battleship in the early 1960s.

the United States lost more than 180 airplanes in the raids.

Japanese losses were comparatively light. About 60 Japanese men died. It is believed that 29 Japanese planes were shot down, although the number might be higher. The Japanese navy also lost five midget submarines and one or two larger submarines.

The attack on Pearl Harbor was shocking. But it failed to deliver the powerful blow that would force the United States to negotiate. None of the U.S. navy's aircraft carriers had been at Pearl Harbor. They all escaped harm. Also, the Japanese bombers had not hit Pearl Harbor's fuel-tank storage area. Destroying these tanks might have forced the U.S. military to retreat to the U.S. mainland for fuel. And Japan had not broken America's will to fight. In fact, it had aroused the country's wrath.

WINNING THE WAR

The attack on Pearl Harbor thrust the United States into World War II. On December 8, President Roosevelt asked Congress for a declaration of war against Japan. He called December 7 "a date which will live in infamy." This phrase has come to refer to the attack on Pearl Harbor.

In his address to Congress, Roosevelt expressed his confidence in the nation's eventual triumph. "No matter how long it may take us to overcome this premeditated invasion, the American people in their righteous might will win through to absolute victory."

Japan's raid on Pearl Harbor had shattered the feeling of isolationism in Congress. Only one member of Congress voted against war. She was Representative Jeannette Rankin of Montana. Rankin was a long-time pacifist who had also opposed America's entry into World War I.

Most Americans abandoned isolationism and dedicated themselves to winning the war. The war, however, would severely challenge the country. On December 11, Japan's allies, Germany and

Jeannette Rankin

36

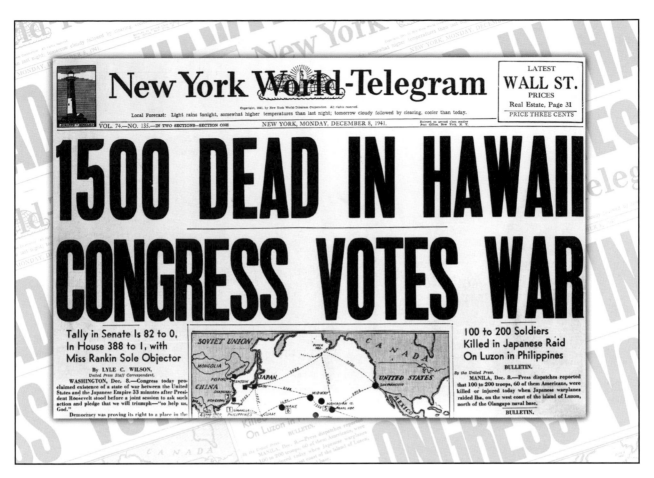

Beneath the declaration of war headline, an article points out that Jeannette Rankin was the only representative to vote against the war.

Italy, declared war on the United States. Congress responded by issuing a declaration of war against Germany and Italy. The United States now faced the prospect of fighting a war in both the Atlantic and Pacific oceans.

The immense task of fighting the war required the United States to harness its resources and people. In 1942, the Roosevelt administration formed the War Production Board (WPB). The purpose of the board was to oversee the country's war mobilization. In addition, the U.S. military was aggressive about acquiring the resources and materials for the war.

The war affected every part of society. Millions of men entered the armed forces, which created a shortage of workers. This shortage was critical at a time when industry needed workers for the war effort. Women offered one source of labor that could be used in the factories. Before the war, many women worked a few years outside the home before they married and then stayed home. Now the government encouraged women to work. About six million women left home to work during the war. Two million of these women took jobs in defense factories.

The woman on this poster by J. Howard Miller became known as "Rosie the Riveter," a World War II icon who encouraged women to enter the workforce.

African Americans also tried to work in U.S. defense plants. However, they faced discrimination when they tried to get these jobs. Finally, African-American leader A. Philip Randolph demanded that President Roosevelt eliminate discrimination at defense plants. In June 1941, the president approved an executive order that banned racial discrimination in these factories. Within a few years, about two million African Americans were working at defense plants.

The amazing industrial capacity of the United States helped the Allies overwhelm Italy, Germany, and Japan. Mussolini's government

JAPANESE-AMERICAN INTERNMENT CAMPS

Within hours of the attack on Pearl Harbor, U.S. security personnel began to round up Japanese Americans. Newspapers accused Japanese Americans of being spies and traitors. In February 1942, President Franklin D. Roosevelt gave the military permission to begin removing Japanese Americans from military locations. More than 100,000 Japanese Americans were forced to move to internment camps.

A U.S. soldier posts an evacuation order.

The Japanese Americans were given a week to sell their homes, businesses, and land and to report for relocation. Many had to sell their properties for much less than they were worth. As they waited to be relocated, Japanese Americans were forced to sleep in poor conditions, sometimes without shelter.

At the 10 internment camps, the Japanese Americans lived in barracks without running water. The camps were surrounded by barbed wire and watched over by guards and snipers. Despite these conditions, the Japanese Americans began rebuilding their lives. They formed sports teams, newspapers, and businesses. Children attended school.

Internment ended in 1945. At the time, many Americans did not believe that it had been wrong to imprison Japanese Americans. It also was not considered strange that German and Italian Americans were not interned.

In 1988, the U.S. government officially apologized for the Japanese-American internment. It called the internment a "grave injustice" and gave money to the 60,000 Japanese Americans still living who had been interned.

Harry S. Truman

Atomic bomb explosion in Hiroshima

collapsed during the war. Germany surrendered to the Allies in May 1945. But it was an important technical development that ended the war with Japan. For several years, the United States had worked on making an atomic bomb. The effort to produce an atomic bomb was called the Manhattan Project.

President Roosevelt did not make the decision to use the atomic bomb in the war. He had died April 12, 1945. Instead, the new U.S. president, Harry S. Truman, decided to use the atomic bomb. U.S. generals had planned an invasion of Japan, but such an attack would be costly. Some estimated that 100,000 U.S. troops would be killed or wounded in the invasion. Truman wanted to avoid these combat casualties.

On August 6, 1945, a U.S. B-29 bomber dropped an atomic bomb on the Japanese city of Hiroshima. The blast killed 70,000 people.

Three days later, the United States used an atomic bomb on the city of Nagasaki. About 40,000 people died in this attack. Thousands of other people died later from burns and illnesses caused by radiation. On September 2, 1945, Japan surrendered to the United States.

The attack on Pearl Harbor had brought the United States into the war. Since then, the country had faced very little destruction on its own soil. The same could not be said of much of the rest of the world. Japan and Germany were in ruins. The United States's allies, Britain and the Soviet Union, had suffered much devastation. In contrast, the United States was by far the richest and strongest country in the world.

The United States quickly assumed global leadership. In 1945, the country helped establish the United Nations (UN). This international organization is dedicated to promoting peace in the world. The meeting that established the goals of the UN was held in San Francisco, California. Later, the UN headquarters was located in New York City, New York.

Although devoted to peace, the United States did not abandon its role as a military leader. In fact, the nation led the effort to contain the Soviet Union. Although the Soviet Union suffered millions of deaths in the war, the country was also powerful. It controlled Eastern Europe and a large part of Germany. U.S. leaders feared the Soviet Union would try to expand its influence. In order to oppose the Soviet Union, the United States formed alliances with other countries.

In the 1930s, the United States had avoided confrontations with Japan and Germany. Americans did not want to become tangled in foreign problems. The attack on Pearl Harbor and World War II transformed the country. America became a leader in both war and peace.

TIMELINE

 1894 to 1895 Japan and China fight the Sino-Japanese War. It ends with the signing of the Treaty of Shimonoseki.

 1898 On February 15, an unexplained explosion sinks the USS *Maine* in Havana, Cuba. This incident leads to the Spanish-American War.

On July 7, the United States annexes Hawaii.

 1904 to 1905 Russia and Japan fight the Russo-Japanese War. It ends with the Treaty of Portsmouth.

 1914 to 1918 World War I is fought in Europe. The United States joins the war in 1917.

 1922 On February 6, the United States, Britain, Italy, France, and Japan agree to the Five-Power Naval Limitation Treaty.

 1929 The Great Depression causes economies around the world to fail.

1937 In July, hostilities break out between China and Japan.

 1939 to 1945 World War II is fought in Europe, Asia, and Africa.

 1941 On December 7, Japanese forces attack Pearl Harbor. The United States enters the war the next day.

 1945 On August 6, the United States drops an atomic bomb on Hiroshima, Japan.

On August 9, an atomic bomb is dropped on Nagasaki, Japan.

In September, Japan surrenders to the United States, ending World War II.

American Moments

FAST FACTS

During the attack on Pearl Harbor, Mess Attendant Second Class Doris "Dorie" Miller came to the aid of his shipmates on the USS *West Virginia*. He helped move the wounded to safety. Afterward, Miller manned an antiaircraft gun until it ran out of ammunition and he was ordered to abandon ship. His actions earned him the Navy Cross. Miller was the first African American to earn this medal.

Of the 21 ships sunk or damaged during the Pearl Harbor attack, only 3 were not repaired and put back into service. These were the USS *Oklahoma*, *Utah*, and *Arizona*. The *Oklahoma* was considered too old to be worth the effort. Long used for practice, the *Utah* was deemed obsolete. Only the *Arizona* was too badly damaged to consider repairing.

The U.S. Navy ships *Bennion*, *Flaherty*, *Frederick C. Davis*, *Herbert C. Jones*, *Hill*, *Kidd*, *Reeves*, *Scott*, *Tomich*, and *Van Valkenburgh* were all named for soldiers who lost their lives during Pearl Harbor. Chief Radioman Thomas J. Reeves actually has two ships named after him. He served on the USS *California*.

The declarations of war against Japan, Germany, and Italy marked the last time that Congress officially declared war. However, the United States has fought in other conflicts since World War II.

In Pearl Harbor, droplets of oil still rise to the surface from the USS *Arizona*. Scientists worry that the oil could cause an environmental disaster. But many are hesitant to stop the leakage. The site of the sunken battleship has become a memorial for the sailors who died in the attack. More than 4,500 people visit the *Arizona* every day.

WEB SITES
WWW.ABDOPUB.COM

Would you like to learn more about the bombing of Pearl Harbor? Please visit **www.abdopub.com** to find up-to-date Web site links about the bombing of Pearl Harbor and other American moments. These links are routinely monitored and updated to provide the most current information available.

Following the Pearl Harbor attack, the USS West Virginia *and the* USS Tennessee *are in flames.*

GLOSSARY

annex: to add land to a nation.

assassinate: to murder a public figure.

asset: something of value. When a government freezes assets, it is stopping the production of the assets.

Buddhism: a religion that was started in India by Buddha. It teaches that pain and evil are caused by desire. If people have no desire, they will achieve a state of happiness called nirvana.

colonialism: one nation having control over the people, resources, and government of another group or nation. Colonized people are dependent on the nation in power.

communism: a social and economic system in which everything is owned by the government and given to the people as needed.

depression: a period of economic trouble when there is little buying or selling and many people are out of work.

dictator: a ruler who has complete control and usually governs in a cruel or unfair way.

discrimination: treating people differently based on characteristics such as race, class, or gender.

executive order: an order given by a country's executive branch.

fortifications: works that are erected to defend a position or place.

loch: a bay that is almost completely surrounded by land.

missionary: a person who spreads a church's religion.

nationalism: a belief by the people of a nation that their culture is superior to other cultures.

pacifist: one who is against using violence to settle conflicts. Pacifists are especially opposed to war.

Shinto: the native religion of Japan. Shinto is marked by worship of nature, respect of ancestors and ancient heroes, and the divinity of the emperor.

telegraph: a system of communication made of wires in which messages are transmitted electronically.

unemployment: lack of a job. The unemployment rate is the number of people in a country that do not have jobs.

whaling: an industry in which whales are hunted for the commercial use of their oil, bones, and other parts.

World War I: 1914 to 1918, fought in Europe. The United States, Great Britain, France, Russia, and their allies were on one side. Germany, Austria-Hungary, and their allies were on the other side. The war began when Archduke Ferdinand of Austria was assassinated. The United States joined the war in 1917 because Germany began attacking ships that weren't involved in the war.

INDEX